40 Days of Biblical & Cultural Insights into the Black Panther Movie

Lisa D. Jenkins

LDJ Ministry & Legacy
East Elmhurst, New York
lisadjenkins.org

For The Millions…

ACKNOWLEDGEMENTS

This book would not have been possible without the encouragement of loved ones.

Blessings and thanks to my executive assistant, Serena Chamblee. You are a gifted gift from God. Words are inadequate for all that you do and your immense help in making sure this project was "up to snuff!"

Special thanks to my sister-in-love, Stephanie Cooper-Smiley, who also proofread and edited this work in record time. If Stephanie doesn't believe in something, she will not be a part of it. Taking on this task was a major motivation because of her faith in the finished project. Thank you, Stephanie.

To the brother God gave me, Cosby B. Smiley, thank you for everything that you do. There's absolutely too much to mention. But thank you especially for marrying Stephanie! :-)

To my son, Jordan Christopher, always believe and keep moving forward. You are already great. Walk into greatness. Receive greatness.

To George Melville Grant, continue healing the world with your compassion and wisdom.

Table of Contents

Preface 9

Day 1 - Third World Notions For First World People: Shake It Off! 13

Day 2 - Don't Freeze." "I Never Freeze." 16

Day 3 - Step Into The Spotlight 19

Day 4 - You Get To Decide 22

Day 5 - We Are Home! 24

Day 6 - This Ends Today! 26

Day 7 - The Protector 28

Day 8 - Now That I Have Your Attention 30

Day 9 - The World Is Changing 33

Day 10 - I Am My Brother's Keeper 36

Day 11 - Your Enemy Is Just Getting Started 39

Day 12 - Humility In High Places 41

Day 13 - A Dora Milaje Mentality 43

Day 14 - You're Just Getting Started 45

Day 15 - The Conquerors 48

Day 16 - A Good Man 50

Day 17 - If It Weren't For The Women 53

Day 18 - God's Reflection 57

Day 19 - It's Your Time 60

Day 20 - A Good Heart 63

Day 21 - The Fierce Urgency of Now 65

Day 22 - Looking for Love In All The Wrong Places 68

Day 23 - The Reason For Your Release 71

Day 24 - Get Suited ______ 74
Day 25 - Yes, I Am New! ______ 77
Day 26 - There's Nothing New About It! ______ 79
Day 27 - One Bad Apple Will Not Spoil The Bunch ______ 82
Day 28 - A War Is Coming ______ 85
Day 29 - Show Them Who We Are! ______ 87
Day 30 - So Primitive... ______ 90
Day 31 - Respect The Throne ______ 94
Day 32 - Take Up Your Shield ______ 97
Day 33 - Let Them Come ______ 99
Day 34 - Cloaked ______ 101
Day 35 - I Shall Not Be Moved ______ 104
Day 36 - Receiving Wise Counsel ______ 107
Day 37 - Ain't I A Woman? ______ 109
Day 38 - I Am A Man ______ 112
Day 39 - The Wait Is Over ______ 116
Day 40 - For The Millions ______ 119
Closing Thoughts ______ 123
About The Author ______ 125

Preface

As a little girl, I would rush to the supermarket checkout counter before my mother made it there with her shopping cart. I knew that there would always be a small wire bookrack with comic books that I could read while my mother was waiting in line. If my mother was in a good mood the comic book would wind up in our shopping cart for me to read on the way home. Usually that was the case because my mother was a firm advocate that any type of reading was good reading. My home was filled with comic books, biographies, science books, black history books, all types of literature and of course bibles. But comic books…! Whether it was Archie Comics, DC Comics or Marvel Comics, it was all good to me. I especially loved the action comics. Even at my young age it was not missed by me that there were few characters with skin that looked like mine. And that mattered.

That's why some 40 odd years later, the Black Panther movie is groundbreaking. The fact that it has taken this long for a movie like this to be made is another story. But I believe that God does things in his own time. I do not think that it is an accident that this movie, full of beautiful black people from the fictional Wakanda in Africa, was released during a period of political chaos where black and brown people are being maligned and marginalized with the blessings of The Administration. The Black Panther is a movie about identity. If humanity, which includes black people, is created in the image of God as referenced in Genesis 1:27, then image is always important. Yes, images of an African country (fictional though it may be) untouched by colonization are important. Images of black women bearing wise counsel as well as strong weapons are important. Images of black men holding their own in a world forced to acknowledge their power are important.

But a bible devotion? For the Black Panther movie? I believe that God is found in everything if we look closely. Rev. Dr. Frederick D. Haynes, pastor of the Friendship-West Baptist Church in Dallas, Texas loves to quote Shakespeare and often says, "sermons are found in stones." If sermons are found in stones, then certainly we can find devotional meditations from a movie that is significant for God's people. I believe that God is always on the side of the oppressed. He is always concerned about the "least of these" as Jesus mentions in Matthew 25:40.

Written and compiled in less than one week with many sleepless nights of prayers and typing, I am excited about this book. I pray that you will be empowered through the words that follow.

DAY 1

Third World Notions For a First World People: Shake It Off!

Genesis 2:10-14 (NRSV) - *A river flows out of Eden to water the garden, and from there it divides and becomes four branches. The name of the first is Pishon; it is the one that flows around the whole land of Havilah, where there is gold; and the gold of that land is good; bdellium and onyx stone are there. The name of the second river is Gihon; it is the one that flows around the whole land of Cush. The name of the third river is Tigris, which flows east of Assyria. And the fourth river is the Euphrates.*

Romans 12:2a (NRSV) - *Do not be conformed to this world, but be transformed by the renewing of your minds…*

One of the things I absolutely love about the Black Panther Movie is its sheer and unashamed blackness. In the film we sec the villain Ulysses

Klaue (aka Klaw) sitting in an interrogation room asking the superhero ally, Everette Ross, if he knows about Wakanda. Ross replies that it's a third world country full of shepherds and people wearing cool outfits. I can't begin to tell you how wrong he is! In the movie, fictional Wakanda is the most technologically advanced place on the planet with the world's most valuable natural resource, vibranium. In the real world, however, it's no secret that much of the western world continues to write off Africans and people of African ancestry as illiterate and backwards when in reality, from the beginning of time, Africa was home not only to humanity, but to philosophers, doctors, architectural engineers and much more. A close examination of the scripture in Genesis gives us the location of the Garden of Eden, which is the birthplace of humanity. When we understand the extent of the rivers mentioned and their most likely original extent deep into Africa, we learn that the Garden of Eden (Hebrew for *paradise* or *pleasure*) is really the Garden of Africa (the word Africa is from Latin). The bible says that the land was full of gold (actually is says "good gold"!) and bdellium or aromatic resin, which was used for medicinal purposes long before there was a

Hippocrates.

So what does this mean for us? While the person sitting in the most powerful seat in the United States, refers to countries filled with beautiful black people as sh*thole countries, remember to be transformed by the renewing of your mind that we are a great people. Shake off the third world notions. God created us in His image and that makes us not just great...it makes us holy. You are holy. Remember that the next time someone tries to tell you that you are something different. You are holy!

Prayer

Lord God, when the world would try to place labels on me that you never intended, please remind me that I am not only loved and beautiful, but that I am holy because I am made in your image. In Jesus' name, amen.

DAY 2

"Don't Freeze." "I Never Freeze."

***2 Timothy 1:7 (NKJV)* -** *For God has not given us a spirit of fear, but of power and of love and of a sound mind.*

There's a scene in the movie where the Black Panther/T'Challa, played by Chadwick Boseman, is suited up and about to slip down his chute and do some superhero stuff. Okoye (played by the Walking Dead's Danai Gurira) is the head of his security team—the oh-so-bad Dora Milaje. Just as T'Challa is about to do his thing, Okoye admonishes him by saying, "Don't freeze." Just before he puts on that oh-so-cool Black Panther helmet, he calmly says, "I never freeze." And then drops down the chute at what we can only assume is the speed of light.

What? Never? If only we could say that. While Okoye admonished T'Challa to not freeze for an entirely different reason, how many times do we allow fear to freeze and paralyze us? Often fear freezes and paralyzes us to the point where we render our own selves unproductive and stagnant. No need to blame anyone else when we've fallen victim to fear. But remember FEAR is simply **F**alse **E**vidence **A**ppearing **R**eal. It has no place in our lives or in God's plan. It is not given by God who has given us power, love, and a sound mind. The two words, *sound* and *mind,* really mean *self-discipline.* God has given us the ability to discipline ourselves and to be ready no matter what comes our way. Remember, fear is an emotion that has no place in the life of God's people. God is telling you "Don't Freeze." Now walk around like the child of God you are and say, "I Never Freeze."

Prayer

God, I know you have not given me a spirit of fear. Therefore, I will be bold in my words, actions and even in my requests. Much of what I do not have is not because you have not planned it for me. It is because I have operated in fear. Help me to claim the inheritance you have laid up for me by ridding my life of fear. In Jesus' name, amen.

DAY 3

Step Into The Spotlight

Genesis 50:19-20 (NRSV)- *But Joseph said to them, "Do not be afraid! Am I in the place of God? Even though you intended to do harm to me, God intended it for good, in order to preserve a numerous people, as he is doing today.*

The music in the background of the trailer for the Black Panther is FIYAH!! Over and over we hear the hook "Step into the Spotlight." While I wouldn't say that the song itself, entitled *Legend Has It*, is child- or work-appropriate, the hook is definitely off the chain! Step into the Spotlight!

Some folk have been languishing in the background of their own lives and in the lives of others for far too long. Perhaps somebody has done you wrong or you have low-self-esteem. No matter. God is saying, "Step Into The Spotlight."

When we look at the story of Joseph in the book of Genesis, we see a man who has definitely been done wrong by others. His own brothers! They considered having him killed but instead sold him into slavery. But God is a table-turner and a script-shredder! He had another plan for Joseph. Years later, the very brothers who sold him into slavery had to come begging for assistance. When they found out that it was Joseph whom they had to approach for help, they were literally frozen with fear. But Joseph calmly said, "Am I in the place of God?" Of course he was! Joseph was in charge and living large. He was in the place God had placed him despite what his brothers tried to do to him. Joseph was in the spotlight.

Where are you? Have you relegated yourself to the sidelines of life or are you ready to step into the spotlight. Know that you are in the spotlight as long as you are in the place of God!

Prayer

Lord, God, I know you have great things in store for me. Please do not allow me to marginalize my own self based upon what others say or do. I am ready to step into the spotlight—not for my sake, but so that you may get the glory. In Jesus' name, amen.

DAY 4

You Get To Decide

Deuteronomy 30:19-20 (NRSV) - *I call heaven and earth to witness against you today, that I have set before you life and death, blessing and curse. Therefore choose life, that you and your offspring may live, loving the Lord your God, obeying his voice and holding fast to him, for he is your life and length of days, that you may dwell in the land that the Lord swore to your fathers, to Abraham, to Isaac, and to Jacob, to give them."*

A poignant moment in the movie is where T'Challa/Black Panther's love interest, Nakia (played by Lupita Nyong'o) says to him, "Only YOU get to decide what kind of king you are going to be." If only more of us would heed such words. God has a calling on each of our lives to do great things. How often and why do we fall short? What kind of choices do we make each day, each minute? From the beginning of time when God told Adam he was free to eat of any tree (well almost any tree) and Adam made the wrong choice, we have seen how our decisions play significant and sometimes detrimental roles in our life journey. Adam blamed his bad choice on the woman and the woman blamed her bad choice on the serpent. The time is up for blaming our problems on others. Certainly there is never a time where we can blame our problems on the Lord. Sometimes we just have to look in the mirror and decide what kind of person we want to be. It's never too late to make that decision. Choose life — not just any life... but a life worthy of a child of the King. You Get to Decide.

Prayer

Lord, God, thank you for giving me life. Now guide not only my heart, but guide my mind and my thoughts. Give me the strength to choose the better part of this world so that I can walk into the greatness to which you have called me. Allow me to not only choose what kind of person I will be, but guide me in the choices I make for those who would be my acquaintances and friends. I believe that I am called for greatness and that you will surround me with greatness, beginning with your son, Jesus. In his name, I pray. amen.

DAY 5

We Are Home

Genesis 28:15a - 16 (NIV) - *"I am with you and will watch over you wherever you go, and I will bring you back to this land." ...When Jacob awoke from his sleep, he thought, "Surely the Lord is in this place, and I was not aware of it."*

After some time in western civilization, T'Challa/Black Panther is on his way back to mythical Wakanda, the richest and most technologically advanced place in the world. Okoye is at the helm of the aircraft when she suddenly declares with a huge smile, "We are home." What do you think of when you think of 'home'? I recall my very first Broadway musical was *The Wiz*. I will never forget Stephanie Mills' Dorothy character singing, "When I think of home, I think of a place where there's love overflowing." And really, that's what home is. Any place where there is love overflowing. The greatest love of all however, is the love that God has for us. In our scripture Jacob has a dream. In his dream, God tells Jacob that he will be with him and he will watch over him. That's love. Overwhelming love. When Jacob wakes up he says to himself, "Surely the Lord is in this place." (v.16.) Notice that Jacob doesn't say that the Lord was in his dream. He says that God is in this place. What place? The place wherever Jacob is...because God has already told him, I am with you and watch over you *wherever* you go. Isn't it good to know that wherever you go, you are at home with God's overwhelming and overflowing love? Thank you God, because wherever you are, I am home!

Prayer

Lord, God I am grateful that wherever I am, you are with me. Therefore, I am home. Please allow your love to overwhelm me in the most beautiful and abundant ways. Allow your love to overflow in my life so that I might know the comfort and contentment of home. Amen.

DAY 6

This Ends Today!

1 Samuel 17:46-47 (NIV) - *"This day the Lord will deliver you into my hands…for the battle is the Lord's, and he will give all of you into our hands."*

The showdown is about to occur with T'Challa/ Black Panther and Eric Killmonger. It is at this point that T'Challa declares, "This ends today!" Notice that he doesn't say it with trepidation or apprehension. He is confident and bold. And that's what David is saying in the 17th chapter of 1 Samuel. Most of us know the story of David and Goliath. The emphasis is usually on the difference in size between the young lad, David, and the giant, named Goliath. But David was also bold when everyone else was fearful. David marched up to the battle line and declared, "This day, the Lord will deliver you into my hands…!" There was no strategy for a long and drawn out battle. David did not map out what he would do over the next few days or how he would get the rest of the army involved. He stood on his own and essentially said, "This ends today!"

What battle are you dealing with where you must step up to the plate and declare "This ends today!"? It's not a request for your worries to be gone. It's not a hopeful plea. It is an assuredness that because of your relationship with God, whatever the enemy has for you, it ends today! Rest easy knowing that the battle is not yours, it's the Lord's and it ends today!

Prayer

Lord, God, give me the boldness and the strength to look the enemy in the face and say, "This ends today!" There are obstacles all around me and they come in various forms. Help me to recognize these obstacles and distractions and declare 'This ends today!' so that I may move forward with your will and your plan for my life. In Jesus' name, amen.

DAY 7

The Protector

***Psalm 91:1-2 (GNT)** - Whoever goes to the Lord for safety, whoever remains under the protection of the Almighty can say to him, "You are my defender and protector. You are my God; in you I trust."*

At the beginning of one of the many advance film trailers we hear Chadwick Boseman's voice in the background saying, "The Black Panther has been the protector of Wakanda for generations. Now it is time to show the outside world who we are."

Psalm 91 is an assurance of God's protection. The psalmist declares that whoever goes to the Lord for safety and whoever remains under the protection of the Almighty can say that God is their defender and protector. A protector is one who guards and defends. This declaration of God's protection is not limited to a certain race or class of people. The bible says *whoever* goes and *whoever* remains. In a world where classism, sexism, racism, and so many other 'isms' are systematically designed to marginalize and oppress certain groups of people, it's great to know that we serve a "whoever kind of God"! A God that will protect anyone who runs to him and acknowledges that he is our protector and our defender. For this we can be grateful.

Prayer

God, I thank you for being my defender and my protector. I thank you for being a 'whoever God". The God who defends and protects whoever will call on you. You are no respecter of person, but you freely shield us from all danger and trouble. Thank you for doing what you do. Thank you for your son Jesus, our friend and intercessor. In Jesus' name, amen.

DAY 8

Now That I Have Your Attention

Luke 1:18-20 (NIV) - *Zechariah asked the angel, "How can I be sure of this? I am an old man and my wife is well along in years." The angel said to him, "I am Gabriel. I stand in the presence of God, and I have been sent to speak to you and to tell you this good news. And now you will be silent and not able to speak until the day this happens, because you did not believe my words, which will come true at their appointed time."*

CIA Operative Everett Ross has been writing off and dismissing the badness and the seriousness of the Black Panther and the people of Wakanda. This is nothing new because we recall in Day One of our devotional, he mistook Wakanda to be a developing, third world country, a common historical mistake (or perhaps a purposeful erasure) that is frequently made by the western world. T'Challa leans down to the sitting level of

Ross and quietly remarks, "Now that we have your attention...." In other words, it had to take a bizarre situation to have occurred for Ross to finally take T'Challa and Wakanda seriously.

Do you ever feel like you're not being taken seriously? Then you can imagine how God feels. God will get ready to position us in a place of wonder, but we're too busy not believing God's "hype." I'm here to tell you, the hype is real! God's hype is always real! In the first chapter of Luke, God sends one of his head honcho angels, Gabriel, to tell Zechariah that he's going to be a father, even though and his wife Elizabeth, are a little up there in age. Zechariah doubts what the angel is saying and Gabriel has to do some flexing. He silences Zechariah. I don't just mean he tells him to 'hush'. He closes the mouth of Zechariah for the entire duration of Elizabeth's pregnancy. I can imagine Gabriel saying, "I just finished telling you that I stand in the presence of God. Now that we have your attention..."

Is God trying to get your attention? Don't wait until he has to discipline you. Listen and watch for his faint but significant signs, wonders and words. They're definitely worth your attention!

* * *

Prayer

God, thank you for taking the time to get my attention. Although I don't always stay alert, I am willing to turn my mind and focus over to you so that you can manage my thoughts. Discipline my mind and keep me ever alert to the magnificent things that you have in store. Keep me alert so that I can know what I am called to do and where I am called to go. With this in mind, I stand ready to be the transformative agent of change that you've called me to be. In Jesus' name, amen.

DAY 9

The World is Changing

***Hebrews 13:8 (NIV)** - Jesus Christ is the same yesterday and today and forever.*

There's an old saying: The more things change, the more they remain the same. So wrong, and yet so true. T'Challa hears the voice of his father, T'Chaka, who is reminding him of the importance of his role as king of Wakanda and its impact on the entire planet. "The World is Changing." No truer words were spoken, even in reality. While many of us have been fighting for progress just as our ancestors did, it seems we have come to a roadblock. November 8, 2016 was a wake-up call that the world is indeed changing for what appears to be the worse, although honestly, it remains the same for poor people, marginalized people, and people of color who are being maligned, disregarded and oppressed.

But the good news is that Jesus Christ is the

same yesterday and today and forever. Jesus came with salvific power to save us from our sins. But he also came to save us from injustice and oppression. In his initial sermon in Luke 4:18-19, Jesus clearly states that the spirit of the Lord is upon him to "bring good news to the poor...and to let the oppressed go free...." This is the Jesus who spoke yesterday and his words stand today and forever. He will always be on the side of the poor and those who the rest of the world maligns. But if we are to be disciples of Jesus Christ, his priorities must be our priorities. In the words of Dr. Obery Hendricks, we must always treat the needs of the people as holy.[1] This is what Jesus does, yesterday, today and forever. He does not change.

Prayer

Lord, God, we thank you for sending your son Jesus Christ who is the same yesterday and today and forever. When so much around us is changing and when people are unpredictable, your Son and

---

[1] Obery Hendricks, *The Politics of Jesus: Rediscovering the True Revolutionary Teachings of Jesus and How They Have Been Corrupted* (New York: Doubleday, 2006), 101

your Word always remain the same and are reliable. Remind us not to rely on those around us but to rely on your son Jesus, the author and finisher of our faith. In Jesus' name, amen.

DAY 10

I Am My Brother's Keeper

Exodus 2:3-7 (NIV) - *But when she could hide him no longer, she got a papyrus basket for him and coated it with tar and pitch. Then she placed the child in it and put it among the reeds along the bank of the Nile. His sister stood at a distance to see what would happen to him. Then Pharaoh's daughter .... saw the basket among the reeds and sent her female slave to get it....Then his sister asked Pharaoh's daughter, "Shall I go and get one of the Hebrew women to nurse the baby for you?" "Yes, go," she answered. So the girl went and got the baby's mother.*

Most of us are familiar with the ageless question, "Am I my brother's keeper?" Cain asked this question in Genesis 4:9, in response to God asking Cain about the whereabouts of his brother, Abel, whom Cain had murdered. I believe it was Cain's indifference and lack of remorse that compounded the sin of his murderous act. However, we see a different story with Miriam and her response to the possible murder of her baby brother, Moses. Pharaoh had put out a death decree on all baby boys, but Moses' mother was determined to save him and Miriam was on board with the plan. After Moses' is set adrift in the river, Miriam looks after him from afar to make ensure that he is alright. Seeing that Pharaoh's daughter has spotted the child and has taken an interest in him, Miriam wisely offers the services of a wet nurse, who just happens to be the mother of Moses...and herself. Miriam was indeed her brother's keeper.

I was reminded of this story because the Black Panther has many strong black women in the film. One of them however, is the very wise and intelligent Shuri, the sister of T'Challa/Black Panther. She is the genius who designed the Black Panther suit and who assists her brother in many ways. She looks after him. She admires him. But let's not get it twisted. It is because of her genius that the Black Panther is a formidable figure to be reckoned with. She is indeed her brother's keeper!

* * *

Prayer

Lord, when so many people are indifferent to one another, let us be mindful that we are indeed the keepers of our brothers and sisters. Let us look for ways to help and to empower one another. Let us not be quick to degrade and demean others. Let us not belittle and cheapen the character of our brothers and sisters. Thank you God for always keeping us. In Jesus' name, amen.

DAY 11

Your Enemy Is Just Getting Started

1 Peter 5:8 (NIV) - *Be alert and of sober mind. Your enemy the devil prowls around like a roaring lion looking for someone to devour.*

Michael B. Jordan's character Eric Killmonger/N'Jdaka is on the mountaintop getting ready for a showdown with T'Challa/Black Panther, when he declares, "I'm just getting started!" Yep. And that's exactly what your enemy is saying. "I'm just getting started!" Because every day there's a new challenge for you. There's a new trial, a new obstacle, and a new test, all designed by your enemy. But the good news is you're ready. You're not ready? Of course you're ready. When you wake up in the morning, just say, "I'm ready!"

The Apostle Peter, in 1 Peter 5:8 admonishes the reader to be alert and of sober mind. Why? Because your enemy is prowling around looking for someone to devour. Peter's instructions are important. Often we get distracted and are not alert. Our mind is not sober or disciplined. And we get side-tracked, and when we are side-tracked we leave ourselves open for the enemy to enter and create havoc in our lives. The enemy is always just getting started. The enemy always has a new trick. A new trap. A new ploy. The enemy always has a game plan to try and trip you up. The enemy is always just getting started. But that's fine. Be sober and be alert. Be woke full-time! So when the enemy comes for you, you can look the devil in the face and say, "Not today! You may be getting started. But I'm already finished!"

Prayer

Lord, I thank you that when the enemy devises plans to come for me, you have already prepared me for the battle. Help me to begin each day knowing that because I am your child, I am a target. But because you are my Protector, it is with your help that I am already the winner. Thank you for continuing to guard me night and day. In Jesus' name, amen.

DAY 12

Humility in High Places

Ephesians 4:2 (NIV) - *Be completely humble and gentle; be patient, bearing with one another in love.*

One of the things that is rare today is to find leaders who sit in high places and who operate from a place of humility. In fact, the opposite is too often true. Too often we are faced with leaders who are narcissistic and who focus on their own welfare and feelings rather than those whom they have pledged to serve. T'Challa/The Black Panther is not just a superhero, but he is the king and the protector of his people. And he is humble. For a long time, no one knew the real identity of him or his father, T'Chaka, and the major role that they play in the lives of their people. While many people in leadership are anxious for publicity and for all to know who they are, it takes humility to operate with quiet strength.

The apostle Paul reminded the Ephesian

people to be completely humble and gentle. Partial or incomplete humility was not an option. He knew that this was necessary for the community to thrive. All of us are leaders in some way or another. Even if we are leading our families or our own lives. We are all leaders. And because we are God's children and joint-heirs with Christ Jesus, we sit in high places. We must remember who we are and to whom we belong. And most importantly, know that whatever we do and whatever we attain, the glory belongs to God who has guided and protected us every step of the way. That's something to be humble about!

Prayer

Lord, God, thank you for seating me in high places. I realize that wherever I am, you are there and with you I am in a high place of love, authority, and assurance. Thank you for opportunities and the ability to influence those around me in positive and magnificent ways. Thank you for the transforming power that you have given me so that I can be a change agent in your kingdom. But, please, Lord, keep me humble. Help me to be patient and to bear with others in love. In Jesus' name, amen.

DAY 13

A Dora Milaje Mentality

***Judges 4:4 (NIV) -** Now Deborah, a prophet, the wife of Lappidoth, was leading Israel at that time.*

Did I tell you that I absolutely love this movie??? Not just the blackness of it all — the ultimate "blackity-black blackness", but the powerful role that women are playing. First, all hail to the real queen, the woman who gives us a new understanding of what it means to be over 60 years of age — Angela Bassett. Also, shout out to Lupita Nyong'o playing the role of Nakia, T'Challa's love interest; Letitia Wright, the Black Panther's sister who has beauty and brains; and certainly a huge shout-out to Danai Gurira who plays Okoye, the general of the Dora Milaje. In case you didn't know, the Dora Milaje is the elite, all-female squad of warriors sworn to protect Wakanda and its king, The Black Panther/T'Challa. In other words, they are BAD, and I LOVE IT!!!

The Dora Milaje remind me of Deborah in the book of Judges. We are introduced to Deborah as a prophet and as a wife. But we are also introduced to her as a leader. And not just any leader. Leaders who are mentioned in the Book of Judges are warriors. They are fit to lead in battle. Deborah commissions the commander Barak to undertake a mission. He is hesitant at first, saying that he will only go to war if Deborah goes with him. Deborah consents. This is an important story because women are often marginalized and viewed as second-class citizens, but the bible clearly indicates where a woman was not only fit for battle, but was *leading* the battle. This was the doing of God. It doesn't matter who you are...God is able to use you. Always know that you are fit for the battle!

Prayer

Lord, thank you for making me fit for the battle. It matters not if I am male or female for your word says in Galatians 3:28 that there is no longer male and female. We are all one in Christ Jesus. Thank you for making me just as I am. I am confident that I am unique and loved and that you are able to do great work through me. Here I am, Lord, send me. In Jesus' name, amen.

DAY 14

You're Just Getting Started

Joel 2:25 (ESV) *- "I will restore to you the years that the swarming locust has eaten, the hopper, the destroyer, and the cutter, my great army, which I sent among you."*

"I'm just getting started." Those are the words of Eric Killmonger, enemy of T'Challa/Black Panther. The words are meant to serve as a warning. But two can play that game. And because we're on the side of our Lord, God, we know who the winner will be. Whatever comes your way, know that you're just getting started. Your latter will always be greater than your former. In our focus scripture, Joel 2:25, God is promising the people that he will restore what has been taken from them. Keep in mind that this declaration from the Lord is after the people had been rebellious and disobedient. God still had mercy on them. He says to the people, "I am going to restore to you the years...."

There had been severe agricultural devastation due to an infestation of insects destroying the crops. The people were suffering in a great way, physically, emotionally and spiritually. But God said I have restoration in store for you. A restoration is pretty much a reset. A reboot. A do-over. Another chance. So whatever you were doing, wherever you are in life, it doesn't matter what anyone says. You can look in the mirror and say, "I'm just getting started!" It's never too late for a new plan. It's never too late for a new journey. You just have to accept the fact that God is merciful. And despite what you've done, who you are, or what the enemy has done, you can say with confidence, "I'm just getting started!"

Prayer

Lord, God, I thank you for a new beginning and the act of restoration. You are a God of second chances and I am grateful for the new mercies I see each and every day. New mercies mean new starts, new revelations, new chances and new miracles. Thank you for allowing me to be a part of this awesome journey that you have orchestrated specifically for me. Give me the ability and wisdom to use my new start to help someone else with their new start. In Jesus name, amen.

DAY 15

The Conquerors

Romans 8:37 (NRSV) - *No, in all these things we are more than conquerors through him who loved us.*

"Soon there will only be the conquered and the conquerors." T'Challa's friend who turned foe, W'Kabi, leader of the Border Tribe makes this declaration at a pivotal moment when the Tribal Council must decide the future of Wakanda. We, too, are often entrenched in pivotal moments when we must make decisions even when our enemies are plotting. It is at these times when it is particularly important to know that because of God's love for us through his son Jesus Christ, we are able to overcome and conquer the worse of situations. But wait. Paul said in Romans that we are *more than* conquerors. What's up with that? Isn't being a conqueror good enough? I've already won. I'm victorious. I'm a conqueror. But to be more than a conqueror? That means that after the win, you really blow the mind of both the enemy and the spectator! You can realize not only your win by conquering your opponent, but you can stand and see them out of your life! You can win, but you can also expect miracles. You are more than a conqueror. So in this world there are indeed the conquered and the conquerors. The great news is that because of Christ and the unfailing love of God, we're always a little "extra"! We don't have to just settle for a victory. We're entitled to a permanent crown. Because we're more than conquerors!

Prayer

Lord, God, thank you for not just allowing me to be a conqueror, but for fashioning my journey and fixing my battles so that I would become more than a conqueror. Remind me, whenever it is necessary, that you are the judge of the race and the battle. I am grateful that even when I do not feel like victory is around the corner, your Word reminds me that you are the judge and your verdict is final. Thank you. In Jesus' name, amen

DAY 16

A Good Man

Matthew 3:17 (NIV) *- And a voice from heaven said, "This is my Son, whom I love; with him I am well pleased."*

Mark 1:11 (NIV) - *And a voice came from heaven: "You are My beloved Son; in You I am well pleased."*

Luke 3:22 (NIV) - *and the Holy Spirit descended on Him in a bodily form like a dove. And a voice came from heaven: "You are My beloved Son; in You I am well pleased."*

It's been said that a good man is hard to find. Not sure how true that is. I believe we are surrounded by lots of good men. We are introduced to one in Black Panther. "You are a good man with a good heart..." says the voice addressing T'Challa. It sounds like the voice of his deceased father, King T'Chaka. We don't see him, but we hear the voice. In the beginning of the gospels of Matthew, Mark and Luke, we have a voice from heaven, the Lord God who references his son by indicating that he is pleased with him. God's loving approval for his son, Jesus occurs right after his baptism by John the Baptist. The baptism was an outward and public statement of his acceptance to the call of his father. Of course, Jesus, being God did not *have* to be baptized. But he did so, in his human form, in order to show obedience to his father and to his calling. He did it to provide an example for us.

These words, uttered by God, can be found in the three synoptic gospels.[2] We witness God the Father speaking fondly of his son, Jesus. We see Jesus himself, the Son. And we have the Holy Spirit present resting upon Jesus. Jesus is now empowered for ministry. Called to do the will of the Father. This should be the calling of every good man — to do the will of the Father.

Prayer

Lord Thank you for good men. Thank you for

---

[2] Synoptic gospels, Matthew, Mark and Luke are called such because the narratives describe events from a similar view. This is opposed to the Gospel of John.

strong men. We thank you most of all for sending Jesus Christ the perfect example of godly men. In Christ Jesus we see faithfulness, we see strength, we see resilience, we see compassion, we see boldness, we see tenacity and we see one who was unafraid to stand up for those who were cast aside. Thank you God, for our savior, your son whom you sent in the form of man. Let us always remember his great sacrifice. In Jesus' name, amen.

DAY 17

If It Weren't For The Women

Luke 24:10 (ESV) - *Now it was Mary Magdalene and Joanna and Mary the mother of James and the other women with them who told this to the apostles.*

The Gospel of Luke is one of my favorite books in the bible because it gives light to women and other marginalized individuals in a way that the other gospels do not. Luke 24:10 highlights a number of women, including Mary Magdalene,[3]

[3] Mary Magdalene is frequently referred to as a prostitute. As recently as Good Friday 2017, I heard a preacher refer to her as a prostitute in his sermon. Absolutely nowhere in the bible does it say that Mary Magdalene is a prostitute. Story tellers, filmmakers and Broadway producers have put a spin on her character for the sake of intrigue. Perhaps because the bible does not mention her as being anyone's wife. However, she was obviously a woman of means because she helped to support the ministry of Jesus. So being a single woman with money means she was a prostitute? Let's squash that fallacy right now. And the next time someone says that Mary

Joanna and Mary the mother of James and their visit to the tomb of Jesus after his crucifixion. The women are the first ones to carry the good news of the resurrection of Jesus Christ. Not all of the disciples believe them at first. But the fact remains that Jesus rose from the dead and the women were the first to bear the good news.

The focus of the Black Panther is, well, the Black Panther, played by Chadwick Boseman. But the fact remains that the storyline would be absolutely nothing without the awesome women (and there are many of them) who support the important storyline. In fact, each of these awesome women is a superhero. A superhero without the title, *superhero.* Okoye, played by Danai Gurira, is the general of the Dora Milaje warriors. Lupita Nyong'o's character, Nakia is the love interest for the Black Panther aka T'Challa, and she is a warrior as well as a world traveler who is somewhat of a spy. The Black Panther's sister, Shuri, played by Letitia Wright, gives credence not only to the fact that intelligence and genius can be one's strength but that women can

---

Magdalene was a prostitute, feel free to give them the side eye.

Also, of note is that Mary Magdalene is the only woman who is mentioned as being present at the tomb in all four gospels.

be mind warriors. And what do we say about the forever regal and forever fly Angela Basset as Ramonda, the mother[4] of T'Challa? She is full of wisdom and pride for her son. She balances the fine line of being his mother and understanding that he is king.

Whether you are a woman or you have women in your life, we must never forget the importance of women in our community. Women have been important in the church, in the civil rights movement, in the quest for freedom from slavery. I can't possibly name all of their names. There are too many who are both known and unknown. But the fact remains, God knows who they are. And you? God knows who you are as well.

Prayer

---

[4] Yes, we know that technically she is the stepmother of T'Challa. But she is often referred to as his mother. This is of special note, because in African societies there is no such thing as stepmother, stepfather, stepchild. Unlike western societies, the family does not use such indicators which weaken the validity of the person's relationship. You're either in or you're not. This was verified on my recent visit to South Africa when I was privileged to attend a braai, hosted by one of our lecturers.

God, the maker of heaven and earth, thank you for the sisters in our lives. While they are often marginalized, misaligned and misused and misunderstood, we know that if it wasn't for the women, your divine plan for our world would not exist. Thank you for the countless women whose names we will never know. The everyday heroes whose victory is often not in being known, but whose victory is often found in their obscurity. In Jesus' name, amen.

DAY 18

God's Reflection

Genesis 1:27 (NRSV) *- So God created humankind in his image, in the image of God he created them; male and female he created them.*

The scripture reference in Genesis 1:27 is known as the Imago Dei — Latin for the image of God. One of the beautiful things about humanity is its diversity. God knew when he created the first man and woman that from them would spring a beautiful creation reflective of his many beautiful and powerful attributes. We often think that we have to alter our appearance in order to fit into society. And it is unfortunate that many societies, communities, schools, workplaces, etc., impose restrictions on individuals, making them conform to the culture of the dominant or privileged group which is in power. These mandates of conformity often compromise one's religion as well as the ability to self-identify as a child of God.

I absolutely love the fact that the characters in the Black Panther movie have a variety of natural hairstyles. Both men and women. I recall reading the comments after an article on the Black Panther and someone noted how he hated Michael B. Jordan's (Eric Killmonger) hair. He felt it was wild and unkempt. Well the word for the day is, "We are not here for you!" Whether you're sporting a style like Kilmonger's cut & locs, Nakia's bantu knots, Queen Ramonda's silver locs, Okoye's bald head, Shuri's braid extensions or T'Challa's conservative lo-fro, allowing him to navigate the western world, you are God's reflection. When we get to heaven I don't believe God is going to ask you about your hairstyle, or even your tattoos or even your piercings. I believe God is going to ask you, did you feed my people who were hungry? Did you clothe those who were in need? Did you speak good news to the poor? Did you fight for those who were oppressed? Did you treat the needs of the poor as holy?[5] This is the true reflection of God and his son, Jesus Christ, as conveyed to us by the Holy Spirit.

---

[5] Treating the needs of the people as holy is mentioned in *The Politics of Jesus: Rediscovering the True Revolutionary Nature of Jesus' Teachings and How They Have Been Corrupted* by Dr. Obery Hendricks

* * *

Prayer

Thank you, Lord, for allowing me to be created in your image. Although the world may try to define me, you are my Creator and you alone are my definer. You continue to remake and remold me into your image—your infinite image. Allow me to celebrate who you have made me to be and to love myself as you love me. You make no mistakes and because of this, I am grateful. In Jesus' name, amen.

DAY 19

It's Your Time

John 19:26-27 (NIV) - *When Jesus saw his mother there, and the disciple whom he loved standing nearby, he said to his mother, 'Dear woman, here is your son,' and to the disciple, 'Here is your mother.' From that time on, this disciple took her into his home.*

The scene opens with Queen Rashonda, played by the Angela Bassett, the inspiration for every woman over the age of 50, reminding us that good days are indeed ahead of us! She looks her son, T'Challa/Black Panther in the eye and says "My son, it is your time." His father has been killed and ready or not, he must assume the responsibility as king and as protector of his people.

Often it is difficult for us to walk in somebody else's shoes. We feel that we can never fill them. I'm sure that the Apostle John felt that way when he stood at the foot of the cross with Mary the mother of Jesus. There he was with Jesus, the savior and his friend hanging on the cross with death edging its way into the scene. But before Jesus breathes his last breath he has a charge for both his mother, Mary, and his friend and disciple, John. To his mother, he refers to John and says, "Here is your son." And to John, he refers to Mary and says, "Here is your mother." I can only imagine what John was thinking. Jesus is telling John that it is his time to be the protector of his mother, the one who gave birth to the Savior, the Living Word. What a task! What a heavy responsibility. The one who raised the Messiah is now the one whom he is to care for.

There is an awesome responsibility that God has for you. It's one that only you can perform. And you may think that you are not ready for it. You may think that you are not prepared or worthy. But God is saying that it's your time. When God gives you the charge, how can you refuse? Be ready. It's your time!

Prayer

Lord God, thank you for calling me to do your

will. Sometimes I feel that I am not ready, but I know that you never make a mistake. Help me to understand my role in your world and help me to never back down from your calling. I accept your charge to be great. In Jesus' name, amen.

DAY 20

A Good Heart

Psalm 51:10-11 (NKJV) *- Create in me a clean heart, O God, and renew a steadfast spirit within me. Do not cast me away from your presence, and do not take Your Holy Spirit from me.*

We hear the voice of 'T'Challa's deceased father saying "You are a good man with a good heart. And it's hard for a good man to be king."

If anyone knew this to be true, it would be David, king of Israel. King David is known as a man after God's own heart.[6] Yes, he was a murderer and an adulterer[7] but somehow he was still able to capture the heart of God. I believe one of the reasons that David was able to capture the heart of God is because he was able to confess his sins and transgressions and ask the Lord to create

---

[6] 1 Samuel 13:14, Acts 13:22

[7] See the narrative in 2 Samuel 11:1-27

in him a clean heart. Psalm 51 is a psalm (song) of cleaning and pardon. It was written by David after the prophet Nathan confronts him about his dirty deeds. David could have dismissed the prophet but instead, he listened to his words and was remorseful and repentant before God. How many times have we done things which were wrong but have not been repentant or remorseful? To be remorseful means we must seek the truth of our actions and to repent means we must perform deeds that will turn us away from our sins.

Regardless of what we have done, it is never too late to ask God to create in us a clean heart and to renew in us a steadfast spirit.

Prayer

Dear Lord, I know that I have done wrong. Not just once or twice, but many times. But I know you are able to create in me a clean heart. I know that you can renew a steadfast spirit that is faithful to you. I thank you that you have not cast me away from your presence and that your Holy Spirit is always available. In Jesus' name, amen.

DAY 21

The Fierce Urgency of Now

Romans 13:11 (NIV) **-** *To this, knowing the time, that it is already the hour for you to awaken from sleep; for now salvation is nearer to us than when we believed.*

Exactly one year before he was to be assassinated in Memphis, Tennessee, Rev. Dr. Martin Luther King delivered a sermon on April 4, 1967 at the Riverside Church in Manhattan. The sermon was entitled, *Beyond Vietnam: A Time to Break Silence.* One of the themes that reverberated in the sermon was the "fierce urgency of now." It wasn't the first time Dr. King mentioned the fierce urgency of now, having declared its importance in 1963 at the March on Washington, DC. Because of the alarming and shamefully oppressive circumstances occurring in the country and in the world—whether racism and the subjugation of the poor or unjust wars and policies across the world

— there is a fierce urgency of now that we must come to grips with. While the scripture for our focus is concerned about being watchful because the end time draws nearer each day, we must not miss that each day we are being held accountable for how we manage the affairs of our lives and the affairs of our communities and our nation.

There is a point where T'Challa/Black Panther declares, "What happens now determines what happens to the rest of the world." While the movie is fiction, no truer words can be spoken today. Many of us living in the United States are keenly aware of the events taking place in our world as a result of the edicts and affronts of the president of our country. We must be aware that God is watching what is happening in our country and the effect it will have on the rest of the world. Many people, Christians in particular, do not involve themselves in politics. I believe involvement in politics is central to the Christian since the policies introduced and passed by our legislative officials directly and indirectly affect the everyday lives of God's people. We must never sit back and allow others to make decisions for us. Each of us must be involved at the local level, if not the national level. Because what happens now, determines what happens to the rest of God's world...and to God's people.

Prayer

Lord, God, your word says that we should pray for those in high places.[8] *Strengthen our resolve so that we may pray for those who enact policies that hurt your people. We pray that their hearts change and that their minds change. We pray that they will realize that you are a God of compassion and that you sent your Son, Jesus to meet the needs of your people. Move us to be involved and not to sit on the sidelines having others made decisions for us. We thank you for the ability to think, to act and when necessary to march and to resist. In Jesus' name, amen.*

---

[8] 1 Timothy 2:1-2

DAY 22

Looking For Love In All The Wrong Places

Romans 5:8 (ESV) - *But God shows his love for us in that while we were still sinners, Christ died for us.*

Black Panther villain Ulysses Klaue (Klaw) is chained in an interrogation room when he tells CIA operative Everett K. Ross that people have been searching all over the world for the precious mineral vibranium.[9] But they realized that the entire time it exists only in Africa. They were looking for something valuable, but in all the wrong places. But what's more valuable than the love of God?

Looking For Love In All The Wrong Places was a catchy country western song that was the theme for the movie *Urban Cowboy* back in 1980. The

[9] Vibramium is the fictional metal used to make Captain America's shield and is found only in Wakanda.

song was about exactly what the title says—looking for love in all the wrong places. We don't have to look far for God's love. It's in Jesus Christ who died for us. The bible says that God shows his love for us even though we are sinners. And he does this through the sacrificial death of his son, Jesus. Notice that the bible does not say that God 'showed' his love for us through the death of Jesus. Rather, he 'shows' his love for us. Even though Christ died once for us, his death is indicative of his consistent love.

Often we look for love in all the wrong places—friends, alcohol, risky relationships, promiscuity, drugs and a host of other 'places' that we use as substitutes for God's love. But know this...we don't need to look any further. God's love is present and it's ready and waiting for us, through His Son, Christ Jesus.

Prayer

Lord, God, I thank you for your Son, Jesus Christ, who is not just an example of your true love for me, but who ***is*** *love. Even as a sinner, I am loved by you. You call me friend and your son Jesus continues to advocate on my behalf. I thank* *you that you think enough of me to love me, even when I do things that are not very lovable. Your love is greater than anything. In Jesus' name, amen.*

DAY 23

The Reason for Your Release

Job 1:13-15 (NRSV) - *One day when his sons and daughters were eating and drinking wine in the eldest brother's house, a messenger came to Job and said, "The oxen were plowing and the donkeys were feeding beside them, and the Sabeans fell on them and carried them off, and killed the servants with the edge of the sword; I alone have escaped to tell you.*

Job 1:17b (NRSV) - *...I alone have escaped to tell you.*

Job 1:19b (NRSV) - *...I alone have escaped to tell you.*

"I'm the only one who has seen Wakanda and made it out alive." So says Ulysses Klaue while being interrogated by Everett Ross. Apparently, he and others visited the advanced nation which has been concealed from the rest of the world, but somehow he made it out. However, instead of accepting the mercy that was given to him, and going on to live a decent, law-abiding life, Klaue is bent on re-entering the country for his own selfish reasons.

But God does not release us from danger so that we can sit on the sidelines. Everyone is saved or released for a reason. In the book of Job we have three servants who have survived three different catastrophes. Job's family and livestock are destroyed, but these three individuals have made it out alive so that they can tell the story of what has happened. The news may not have been good news for Job who lost everything, but the three survivors are witnesses to what has happened (tragedy) and to what is possible (escape). After much debate with God and with friends, Job later has his family and fortunes increased. But it was three unnamed individuals who escaped from terror that were witnesses to Job about happened. It might seem like they were witnesses only to tragedy. But without the tragedy, Job would never have known the triumph.

If you think back over your life, there were some times when you should not have survived, but today, you're a survivor. And not only are you a survivor, you have been released for a reason! Do not let your past tragedies confine you to the sidelines. Remember, God has something great for you. You have been released for greatness! That's major!

Prayer

Lord, God, Creator and Giver of life. Thank you for making a way. Thank you for making me a survivor. Because you allowed me to survive I will never take life for granted. I know that you have given me a purpose. Allow me to witness to others about your great mercy and your awesome grace. Allow me to be the light and to never take life for granted. In Jesus' name, amen.

DAY 24

Get Suited

Ephesians 6:10-11(NIV) - *Finally, be strong in the Lord and in his mighty power. Put on the full armor of God, so that you can take your stand against the devil's schemes.*

One of the things that's unique about the Black Panther's suit is that it's not just completely bulletproof, but it also absorbs energy. But it doesn't *just* absorb energy. Rather, the absorbed energy is redistributed throughout the entire suit and strengthens the Black Panther as well as the suit that he's wearing. In other words, bullets don't just bounce off of the suit. Bullets make the suit stronger.

In the book of Ephesians, Paul gives a directive to the Christian to get suited up and put on the full armor of God in order to stand against the schemes of the devil. Putting on armor is the first step prior to stepping into battle. Paul urges the

Christian to put on *God's* armor for battle. In other words, the armor is not ours to choose. It's the Lord's armor — the only armor able to withstand the enemy. The verse also lets us know that when we put on the armor, we are not to attack or to advance against the adversary. Instead once we are suited up we are to stand and hold our ground despite the schemes and strategies. It is not a physical struggle like we see in action films like the Black Panther. The struggle is a spiritual one.

Too often we try to fight the battles of this world ourselves. But God is saying that if put on the whole armor—his armor—as found in verses 14-17, and pray in the Spirit as indicated in verse 18, all we need do is stand and let the Lord fight our battle. Aren't you tired of fighting anyway? It's time to be a good soldier and follow God's instructions and let him handle your fight. It's a guaranteed victory!

Prayer

Lord, thank you for being my Commander-in-Chief. I am sorry that I've tried to fight battles on my own. I am strengthened by your might and by your power. I now realize that all I have to do is put on your armor, as indicated in your word, and stand. I know you will do the rest. Thank you for taking charge of my battles. In Jesus' name, amen.

DAY 25

Yes, I'm New!

2 Corinthians 5:17 (NRSV) - *So if anyone is in Christ, there is a new creation: everything old has passed away; see, everything has become new!*

"This movie looks so different and new!" So said a movie critic in reference to the Black Panther film. Yes, it does, because it's full of gorgeous black people who come from a place in Africa that has not been touched by colonization. It is not a third world country or a developing country. It is an advanced country that is far more developed than any place on the earth. It is certainly different and it is certainly new. But, most important, it is about time!

I believe that God sometimes says that about us. "It's about time!' Sometimes God is calling out to us, but we ignore His call. But when we finally accept His son, Jesus as our Savior, we are new creations. And God is saying "It's about time!" The bible says that not only are we new creations, but old things have passed away and everything has become new. What *was*, is no more; and what *is*, is something brand spanking new. When we accept Jesus as our Lord, that's when folk can look at us and say, "Your life looks so different and NEW!" And you can look them in the eye and say, "Yes, it is! I am a new creation. I'm fashioned by God. I am his handiwork. He has *re-formed* me with his hand of divinity and I am not only new, I'm better! I'm freer, I'm stronger, I'm wiser, I'm smarter! I am new! And it's all because of Jesus Christ!"

Prayer

Dear God, Creator of heaven and earth and Creator of humanity. I confess that I have not always acknowledged you as the one who creates and re-creates. But with your son Jesus in my life as my savior, I know that I am a new creature. Thank you for not leaving me the way I was. Because of you I have a new life and I am able to start over. Thank you. In Jesus' name, amen.

DAY 26

There's Nothing New About It!

Ecclesiastes 1:9-10 (NRSV) - *What has been is what will be, and what has been done is what will be done; there is nothing new under the sun. Is there a thing of which it is said, "See, this is new?" It has already been, in the ages before us.*

This movie looks so different and new!" So said a movie critic in reference to the Black Panther film. Wait. This sounds familiar. We just finished talking about how wonderful it is to be a *new creation* because of our relationship with Jesus Christ. But now we read that there is *nothing new* under the sun. Confused?

This passage of scripture, which many believe was written by King Solomon, reminds us that even though new events occur, there is still a cycle and repetition of events — both natural and those accomplished by humans. Someone may climb a mountain and someone else may dive into the great ocean. They are both journeys which involve adventure and risk. Nothing new. Someone discovers dynamite, while someone else later discovers the hydrogen bomb. Different events, but still each is a discovery. Nothing new.

So even though we have new technology to help us do things more quickly and efficiently, we are still doing the same things. We board jets to help us reach our destinations more comfortably and in record time, but we are still reaching destinations.

And so, while many people are saying that the Black Panther movie is so different and new, it really isn't. Black people have always been superheroes. Many of us need look no further than our parents. Despite not having much of any formal education because of the segregation in the south and the poverty which forced many of our fore-parents to work at young ages to help support their families they were able to leave legacies. Black people have always prospered. Just look at Tulsa, Oklahoma in the early 1900s, which was known as Black Wall Street. Because the black residents were prosperous and independent, racist segregationists burned the town to the ground. But our people have always done great things. Nothing new about it!

And today, our sheroes and heroes are continuing to fight and prosper and hold on.... by the grace of God...there's nothing new about what we do!

Prayer

Thank you, Lord, that even though your word says that you make all things new[10]*, there are some things that remain consistent. Thank you for the legacy of our ancestors who survived in spite of great challenges and for the many individuals who today survive in spite of great challenges. They are our superheroes, the marvelous ones. When we are weary of the hurdles of this world, remind us that we are the legacy of superheroes and that with you, God, all things are possible. In Jesus' name, amen.*

[10] Revelation 21:5

DAY 27

One Bad Apple Will Not Spoil the Bunch

Acts 1:24-26 (NRSV) - *Then they prayed and said, "Lord, you know everyone's heart. Show us which one of these two you have chosen to take the place in this ministry and apostleship from which Judas turned aside to go to his own place." And they cast lots for them, and the lot fell on Matthias; and he was added to the eleven apostles.*

Rotten Tomatoes is a review website for film and television. The website staff collects reviews from writers who are certified members of various writing guilds and film critics associations. For a real good minute, Black Panther had a perfect 100% Fresh Score on Rotten Tomatoes, meaning that writers and critics had given it raving 4-star reviews. But then it happened. One writer, Ed Power, of the Irish Independent, found fault with the movie because... (Are you ready?) Apparently the critic took issue with the Black Panther's attempt to uplift meaningful themes in the movie rather than display an abundance of violence. Yep. Not enough black-on-black violence for this critic. No. For real. Here are his exact words:

> *"What he doesn't get to do much of is jump around beating up bad guys. That's a shame. Marvel has finally given us an African superhero. The hope surely was that he would be allowed do superheroic things."*

What's really a shame is that this writer's definition of "heroic" is consistent with violence and beating up people. The fact that Black Panther is a film that places ethics, wisdom and ingenuity on a high plane is obviously bothersome to some. Since Power's less-than-perfect review was published, he has been joined by one more critic. Still one bad apple will not spoil the bunch.

We know the story of Judas, one of Jesus' trusted disciples, who betrayed him and who later hung himself. In the Book of Acts (The Acts of The Apostles), the remaining 11 disciples prayed for a replacement for Judas. We see that the Lord showed them that Mathias was to be added to the group. We find no further information about Matthias in the New Testament. The simple fact that we know God used Matthias to replace Judas is evidence that one apple doesn't spoil the bunch or as the folk would say back in the day, 'one monkey don't stop no show.'

So don't be discouraged when folk disappoint you. God always has a Plan B, and God's Plan B, is always better than our Plan A.

Prayer

God, thank you that even though disappointments come our way, you are always ready to provide whatever is needed in our lives. We know that no matter what others expect of us, you will always show us what is right. Help us to not conform to the levels that this world expect of us. Help us to soar to new heights. Infuse in us the values and ideals that exemplify integrity and give us a moral compass that points toward greatness. In Jesus' name, amen.

DAY 28

A War Is Coming

2 Chronicles 20:15 (NIV) - *He said: "Listen, King Jehoshaphat and all who live in Judah and Jerusalem! This is what the Lord says to you: 'Do not be afraid or discouraged because of this vast army. For the battle is not yours, but God's.*

"A war is coming!" declares Eric Killmonger, played by Michael B. Jordan. And yes Killmonger, along with Ulysses Klaue, is bringing on the heat. A war is definitely coming!

Same thing for us. We have wars, battles, conflicts and struggles. Everyday there is something new to confront. And it often seems like you're outnumbered. But in 2 Chronicles there is a somewhat obscure guy named Jahaziel who was used by the spirit[11] and who spoke a great word of encouragement to King Jehoshaphat, who was

[11] 2 Chronicles 20:14

about to go into war. "Do not be afraid....The battle is not yours, but God's."

How often do we worry about the battles in life, both great and small? The fact remains that we will always have conflicts. We will always wrestle with challenges. But if we know in advance that the battle is God's battle, we should be able to confront the situation with a calm mind and with a spirit of steadfast confidence. Studies have shown that the boxer with the most confidence is the one who usually wins the fight. Not the most skilled. Not the strongest. The one who enters the ring without a shadow of a doubt that he will win. This is what made Muhammad Ali the greatest of all time.

So yes, a war is coming. But God is already on the battlefield! That's more than good news!

Prayer

God. you are my fortress and in you alone do I trust. I thank you for covering me and protecting me. When strife and struggles come, I know you will fight my battles. I willingly step aside so that you can take center stage in my life and on the battlefield. I know that with you there is only victory! In Jesus' name, amen.

DAY 29

Show Them Who We Are

Matthew 5:16 (NRSV) - *In the same way, let your light shine before others, so that they may see your good works and give glory to your Father in heaven.*

As we've mentioned earlier, the fictional country of Wakanda has been hidden from the western world. Its resources have been protected and the genius of its people have propelled the nation into a technological marvel. But as we just learned, a war is coming. And now T'Challa/Black Panther has made the decision. "Let's show them who we are." Yep! Folks' minds are about to gct blown!! They're just not ready! They're just not ready!

And you know what? The same thing goes for you, my friend. When you accept Jesus, the Spirit of God operates in you as a light that shines so that others can know you for who you are. A child of God. A child of the King. Your past doesn't matter. What others think of you doesn't matter. All that matters is that when you truly accept Jesus and when you truly decide to be his disciple, the light in you cannot help but shine before others. And when it does they will see the good works which are manifested by the Holy Spirit. And it's all for the glory of God, our Father in heaven. Understand, good works do not get us into heaven. But if we are true disciples, we produce good works naturally as a result of the Holy Spirit who was sent by God through His son Jesus.[12]

So don't be afraid to show folk who you are. It's not showing off. It's not being boastful. Folk may not be ready for the new you. But you're about to blow their minds! With humility and grace, let the world know who you are so people can glorify your Father who is in heaven!

Prayer

Lord, I thank you for your Holy Spirit which allows your new light to shine in me. Thank you that even though some might have expectations of

---

[12] John 14:26

me that are contrary to who I am in Christ Jesus, you continue to let my light shine. Your word says that the light of a lamp is never under a bowl, but always on a stand in order to give light to the entire house.[13] *Please give me the ability to give light to the world so that people might know you and glorify you. In Jesus' name, amen.*

[13] Matthew 5:15

DAY 30

So Primitive

2 Corinthians 10:3-5 (NRSV) - *Indeed, we live as human beings, but we do not wage war according to human standards; for the weapons of our warfare are not merely human, but they have divine power to destroy strongholds. We destroy arguments and every proud obstacle raised up against the knowledge of God, and we take every thought captive to obey Christ.*

The war is now raging in the Black Panther. The battle is on. And Okoye, head of the all-female Dora Milaje security unit, along with Nakita, is in hot pursuit of Klaue in a thrilling car chase. With Nakita driving, Okoye derisively mocks their opponents with the statement, "Guns. So primitive." It's an interesting statement given the high rate of gun violence in the United States. As of October 31, 2017, we were ranked 31 among countries world-wide for deaths due to gun-violence. That's significant.[14] Even more poignant is that just two days prior to the release of Black Panther, 17 innocent victims of Stoneman Douglas High School in Parkland Florida were gunned down because of inadequate gun regulations.

The irony with Okoye's statement regarding the primitive use of guns by their opponents is that Africa has long been viewed by many in the western culture as a primitive continent. But we see exactly the opposite in the Black Panther movie. Instead of guns, the Dora Milaje uses martial arts, which requires superb mental focus. The weapons used by the Dora Milaje and the rest of the Wakandans are not conventional. But they are more than sufficient.

As Christians we have weapons that are not conventional. The Apostle Paul tells us in 2 Corinthians that the weapons of our warfare are not human. They are not made by conventional methods used by humans. But our weapons are

---

[14] https://www.npr.org/sections/goatsandsoda/2017/10/06/555861898/gun-violence-how-the-u-s-compares-to-other-countries

divine and they have the power to destroy the strongholds of this world. The bible says that our weapons destroy arguments and obstacles, which are opposed to everything that God stands for. Our weapons can destroy strongholds such as poverty, racism, violence, brutality, discrimination, homophobia, xenophobia, apathy, mediocrity and more. And, of course, we all have our own personal strongholds in our lives. But we have the weapons of prayer, fasting, meditation and scripture reading. We also have the disciplines of positive fellowship and our ability to operate with integrity each day.

All of these are weapons that the enemy does not want us to use. They require a level of discipline that is far above what Satan would have us to do. But we're not on Satan's side, are we? No, we take our marching orders from the Lord. And our weapons are from His armory.

Prayer

Lord, God, thank you for being the Commander of our army and of my life. Thank you for supplying weapons which are not formed and fashioned according to human standards. We are grateful for weapons which have divine power to destroy the strongholds in our lives and in this world. Remind us that the battle is yours and that if we hold our ground and obey your commands, we will be victorious! In Jesus name, amen.

DAY 31

Respect The Throne

***Hebrews 12:2 (NRSV)** - …looking to Jesus the pioneer and perfecter of our faith, who for the sake of the joy that was set before him endured the cross, disregarding its shame, and has taken his seat at the right hand of the throne of God.*

Respect the throne. This is one of the latest catchphrases for the Black Panther trailers. It's a reminder that the villains, no matter what kind of power they think they have, must respect the fact that the superhero Black Panther is also king of a great nation, full of great people. Respect the throne, baby. Don't get it twisted.

And for us? Yep. Respect the throne. THE throne. The writer of Hebrews is encouraging the people to continue running the difficult race called life. In verse 1, he has already mentioned the ancestors, the great cloud of witnesses. This is an encouragement that the ancestors are the witness and testimony to the infinite possibilities of God's people. And now the writer is telling the people in Hebrews 12:2 to fix their eyes on Jesus. It appears that he must give them this advice because their eyes were fixed elsewhere, other than on Jesus, the one who endured the cross for us. All too often we lose sight of what is important. We fix our eyes and our attention on people and things that distract us from our goals. And then we fall into depression when we miss the mark. However, the bible says that our eyes are to stay on Jesus who has sat down at the right hand of the throne of God. I like the New Revised Standard Version translation because it says that Jesus has "taken his seat." He has not merely sat down in a seat. He has taken *his* seat right there next to the throne of God, his Father. And because we are joint-heirs with him, we too have the seat of royalty!

Prayer

God thank you for your son Jesus, the author and finisher of my faith. Remind me to focus and fix my eyes on him and him alone. I know that Jesus endured the cross for me and is now sitting at the right hand of your throne. Let me never forget that you are my Protector, my Ruler and my King. In Jesus' name, amen.

DAY 32

Take Up Your Shield

Ephesians 6:16 - (NRSV) - *With all of these, take the shield of faith, with which you will be able to quench all the flaming arrows of the evil one.*

There are at least two types of shields mentioned in the bible and known to ancient soldiers. The small round shield which we often see in movies and the larger oblong shield which covered and protected much of the soldier's entire body. It was usually about four feet in height and about two to three feet in width. The idea is that a shield of faith is one that will protect the Christian from the dangerous arrows of the evil one, whom we assume to be Satan. Many theologians believe that the fiery arrows of the evil one represents various forms of wicked speech aimed at God's people. Whatever the fiery arrows represent, they are no match for the shield of faith. Faith is believing and knowing beyond a shadow of a doubt that you have God to protect you, even when you feel alone and see no evidence.

Faith is a shield stronger than anything; even stronger than the shield of Captain America. What does Captain America's shield have to do with the Black Panther and what does it have to do with you and me? His shield is made of vibranium, which is only found in Wakanda. And while we're not yet sure how the vibranium was taken from the reclusive country of Wakanda and placed into Captain America's shield, we are certain that there is no defensive weapon that is stronger...at least in the fictional Marvel world of superheroes such as the Black Panther and Captain America. But we live in the real world, where faith is real and where God is real. So when you get suited up as we mentioned on Day 24, don't forget your shield of faith. Don't leave home without it!

Prayer

Lord, when we rise daily, remind us to take up the shield of faith. So much is happening in our world but we know that when we are equipped with your armor, no weapon formed against us will prosper. Thank you. In Jesus' name, amen.

DAY 33

Let Them Come

Psalm 27:3 (CEV) - *Armies may surround me, but I won't be afraid; war may break out, but I will trust you.*

Psalm 27 is known as a triumphant psalm of confidence. It's one thing to be confident when everything is going well and you are surrounded by friends and loved ones. It's an entirely different story to be confident when you are surrounded by enemies. But that's just what the psalmist and king, David, is. Confident. Even though armies may surround him, he declares that he will not be afraid. Even though war is imminent, he will trust in the Lord.

T'Challa references his enemies and firmly states, "Let them come." He is unafraid. He is confident because he knows who he is, he knows the type of army he has and he knows the type of weaponry and mastery of martial arts at his disposal. It doesn't matter what the enemy has. He is not concerned.

What a lesson for us. We're often busy trying to figure out what the enemy has so that we can come up with our own strategies. But if we trust in the Lord, we won't have to worry. We can say, "Let them come." Leave it to the Lord, and he will handle everything.

Prayer

Lord, I put my trust in you and you alone. When enemies and armies surround me, I will not be afraid and I will not fear. I know that your word says that you have not given me a spirit of fear, but of power and of love and of a sound mind.[15] *Help me to lean on you and your Word, knowing that I am always safe in your arms. In Jesus' name, amen.*

---

[15] 2 Timothy 1:7

DAY 34

Cloaked

Luke 8:17 (NIV) - *For nothing is hidden that will not be disclosed, nor is anything secret that will not become known and come to light.*

A great crowd had gathered around Jesus and he began speaking parables to them. I remember as a young girl in Sunday School learning that a parable was an "earthly story with a heavenly message." It was supposed to be a story that we could relate to so that we would understand God's purpose in our lives and His reason for sending His son Jesus to us. I'm not sure if they still teach that in Sunday School nowadays, but I never thought that the stories Jesus told were very earthly. I mean, I never thought that they had anything to do with my life — bushels and lamps under jars and lamps on lampstands, jars under the bed, seeds being sown on stony ground. None of this made any sense to me. It was many years later that I realized that the words or parables spoken by Jesus were addressed to individuals who lived thousands of years ago in an agricultural society with no electricity for light bulbs and no running water that could be poured into a glass and placed on a kitchen table. But even though the context was different, the message can certainly be applicable.

Nothing is hidden that will not be disclosed.[16] The parable was meant for the disciples of Christ to know that there will come a time when the good news of Jesus Christ must be revealed and brought to the light. Nothing great can be concealed forever.

So it is in the mythical kingdom of Wakanda, a place untouched by colonization —concealed and hidden from the rest of the world and with its resources safe and secure. But nothing can be concealed forever. How will we respond to the revelation of whatever is precious and rare and good? Some things which have been obscure in our lives are nearer than we know. What is nearer than you know that God is waiting to reveal? Pray about it. And allow God to manifest great things in

---

[16] Luke 8:17a

your life!

Prayer

Lord, your word says that nothing is hidden that will not be disclosed and that anything that is secret will eventually be known and come to the light. I thank you in advance for your divine mysteries which you make known to those who love you. I ask that you keep me in a position to be receptive to your light and to your will. In Jesus' name, amen.

DAY 35

I Shall Not Be Moved

Exodus 14:13 (NRSV) - *But Moses said to the people, "Do not be afraid, stand firm, and see the deliverance that the Lord will accomplish for you today; for the Egyptians whom you see today you shall never see again.*

There's an old Negro Spiritual[17] which goes, "I shall not, I shall not be moved. I shall not, I shall not be moved. Like a tree planted by the waters, I shall not be moved." The song was later used during the civil rights movement and the pronoun "I" was changed to "we". It was a collective statement of resistance during the Jim Crow era where the law of segregation ruled the south while

---

[17] Many people prefer to use the term African-American spiritual. I prefer to continue using the term "Negro" because I feel it evokes a unique ethos that enables us to connect with our ancestors who struggled to survive in the United States of America.

the subtle and not-so-subtle practice of discrimination and racism prevailed in the rest of the country.

We've seen the indigenous people in our country—people known as Native Americans—take stands in order to protect their sacred land. They, too, sing "We shall not be moved." Even though T'Challa/Black Panther is a fictional character, it is easy for one to identify with his passion when he stands for what he believes is fair and right. He would/could not be moved.

And so Moses tells the Israelites who have escaped from the bondage of Egypt, "Do not be afraid, stand firm..." The Israelites are scared because the Egyptians are fast on their trail, pursuing them. They are hemmed in by the Red Sea with what appears to be no way of escape. But the problem is that they were looking back at the Egyptians — the very ones whom they were running from. Moses tells them to see the deliverance that the Lord will accomplish. That might have been a challenge because they had not yet been delivered. But they needed to believe that deliverance was at hand. God did not bring them that far to leave them.

God did not bring you this far to leave you. He

will always open up the sea in front of you and provide a way of escape. You may not see deliverance with your eyes, but I encourage you to see deliverance with your faith. Your rescue party is on the way!

Prayer

Lord, I thank you for placing wise people in my path. Help me to recognize and discern who is for you and who is not for you. Help me to discern who you would have me to listen to. I know that if I plan on my own I will fail, but if I listen to the counsel that you send my way, I cannot fail. In Jesus, name, amen.

DAY 36

Receiving Wise Counsel

***Proverbs 15:22 (ESV)** — Without counsel plans fail, but with many advisers they succeed.*

How many times do we fail simply because we refuse to listen to wise counsel? How often do we think we know everything, only to realize that we really didn't know as much as we thought we did? The duty of a leader is to surround herself or himself with individuals who will provide wise counsel and give good advice. It's been said that you are only as good as the people you surround yourself with. And while the protagonist in our film of focus for this devotional might be the king who is charged with leading and protecting the people of Wakanda, he is not beyond receiving counsel from those around him. This is particularly true with regard to the women in his life. Whether it is from his mother, Queen Romanda, Okoye who heads up the elite all-female warrior unit, his sister, Shuri, or his love interest,

Nakita, T'Challa realizes that he will not be able to lead on his on without wise counsel.

The bible is clear with this one verse, "Without counsel plans fail, but with many advisers they (plans) succeed." Be careful with whom you surround yourself. Ask God to send wise friends and colleagues who you can learn from so that you can succeed and be the best God has called you to be. God's kingdom needs you!

Prayer

Lord, I thank you for placing wise people in my path. Help me to recognize and discern who is for you and who is not for you. Help me to discern who you would have me to listen to. I know that if I plan on my own I will fail, but if I listen to the counsel that you send my way, I cannot fail. In Jesus, name, amen.

DAY 37

Ain't I A Woman?

John 4:7 (NRSV) *- Samaritan woman came to draw water, and Jesus said to her, "Give me a drink."*

At the 1851 Women's Rights Convention in Akron, Ohio, Sojourner Truth gave her famous speech, "Ain't I A Woman?" In this speech, she articulated her identity in a manner that demanded the respect and liberty that were due to her as a child of God. At first there were questions about whether she should speak, since the organizers of the Women's Rights Convention did not want to confuse abolitionism with suffrage. But because of Sojourner Truth's ability to capture the attention of audiences, the organizers relented. The question, "Ain't I A Woman?" reverberated in the hearts of those who heard her and was transcribed and printed by various reporters with many different versions currently existing.

The story of the Samaritan woman, in the 4th Chapter of John, is a story about Jesus approaching a woman who many during that time would not have spoken to. But Jesus always does the unconventional. Not only does he ask her for a drink of water, but he engages her in a theological conversation. Even though she is a Samaritan,[18] and a woman, Jesus still approaches her and opens up dialogue. He ignores her gender and opens up a discussion with her; after her arguing with the Savior, Jesus convinces her that he is the long-awaited Messiah. She then becomes an evangelist, telling everyone about her encounter with the Messiah.

The Black Panther movie is filled with women who have many gifts. I'm not sure if these women would be acknowledged for who they are outside of the fictional Wakanda, but it's admirable that the producers placed emphasis on those special gifts. It is my prayer that one day we can get to the place where one half of God's creation will never have to ask the question, "Ain't I a woman?"

---

[18] Samaritans had mixed blood and were looked down upon by many Jews of the time.

* * *

Prayer

God, we thank you for the phenomenal women in our lives as well as those who have gone before us. Women who have been bold and courageous despite the many challenges of gender and race. We celebrate their tenacity and their strength — mothers, wives, sisters, daughters, aunts, and friends. We ask for your protection around the wonderful women in our lives, while you continue to build and raise them up, and point them in the path of an egalitarian society filled with respect. In Jesus, name, amen.

DAY 38

I Am A Man

Judges 11:2-3 (NIV) - *Gilead's wife also bore him sons, and when they were grown up, they drove Jephthah away. "You are not going to get any inheritance in our family," they said, "because you are the son of another woman." So Jephthah fled from his brothers and settled in the land of Tob, where a gang of scoundrels gathered around him and followed him.*

February 1, 1968: two African-American Memphis sanitation workers, Echol Cole and Robert Walker, were crushed to death after seeking shelter from a storm in the back of the sanitation truck compactor which "malfunctioned." Black workers were not allowed to ride in the truck cabin with the white workers. Frustrated by the city's response to this latest tragedy in a long list of events, over 1300 black men went on strike. If you've not already seen the powerful and compelling photographs of Black men carrying signs saying "I Am A Man," a quick internet search will help you understand. It's a bit of history everyone should know. The strike and the marches were even more riveting because of the unity and the dignity of the men. Each man was well-dressed and each one carried a sign with the same, exact black and white wording—"I Am A Man."

The African-American men in Memphis were somewhat like Jepthath. They were looked down upon and deemed unworthy until those in power needed something from them. After being banished from his home by his own brothers, I can see Jepthath in my imagination declaring, "I Am A Man." He may not have had the same mother as his brothers, but he was still God's warrior and God's man. We see how sooner or later, there must be a realization that often the ones we cast aside are the very ones God will use for victory. So it was with Jepthath.[19] He was ridiculed and ostracized by his own family, but folk soon had to reach the conclusion that if they

[19] Chapters 11 and 12 in the Book of Judges give a detailed account of Jepthath's victories. He is more famous, however, for his rash and reckless vow which led to the death of his only daughter.

were to win the battle against their enemies then Jepthath was the man who would have to lead them.

Still today, African-American men are enduring the challenges of being Black in America. Just a few years ago many were rejoicing because they felt that we were finally in a post-racial society. However, any foolhardy sentiments of a post-racial society have now been washed away with the reality that we are living in a country that has been waiting to resurrect the ugly head of racism.

I celebrate the movie the Black Panther not just because I think it is a great action movie. I celebrate it because the lead character, the protagonist, doesn't have to walk around with a sign that says, "I Am A Man." He simply has to walk. And before he even opens his mouth, we know who he is. To the millions of brothers who never get the spotlight. We see you. We celebrate you. We love you. We're praying for you.

Prayer

God, we thank you for strong black men. For brothers who endure discrimination in our country and in our world. We ask that you strengthen them and give them the fortitude to move forward even when others create policies and strategies designed to marginalize them. We ask that you fortify them for the road ahead and for the sake of their families and their communities and our collective future. In Jesus' name, amen.

DAY 39

The Wait is Over

1 Peter 4:7 (NIV) - *The end of all things is near. Therefore be clear-minded and sober, so you can pray.*

The final commercials and trailers for Black Panther have been released. After the hyped music and the stunning graphics you see the giant words in a grey granite rock font pop onto the screen — THE. WAIT. IS. OVER.

Yes, the wait is over. The countdown has begun. We're down to the wire. Are we there yet? Almost! Most of us can't wait to get into the theatre with our bag of popcorn. Extra butter please and thank you!

1 Peter 4:7 is also telling us that the wait is over. This advance notice given by Peter is a bit gloomier than the commercial spots done by the advertising agency hired by the Black Panther folk. It starts off by saying "The end of all things is

near." Yikes! But let's be clear. Honestly, the ends of all things really *is* near, comparatively speaking. When we're talking about millions of years of the earth spinning, the end really is *kinda* near, and let's face it, each of us has an appointed time to meet our maker. It's a fact that we often don't want to talk about, but it is inevitable. The bible says therefore, be clear-minded and sober, so you can pray. The question one might ask is, "Can't I pray to God no matter what condition I'm in?" Sure. But Peter is saying that because every minute is precious, we really would want to remain clear-minded and sober so that our prayers are targeted to heaven with clarity and specificity. This is no time for vague ramblings. The time is too important and the moment is too urgent. The wait is over my beautiful people. Now is the time to pray, act, resist, advocate and work. The question has been asked: *If not you, then who? If not now, then when?*

Prayer

Lord, God, we know that each minute we breathe draws us closer to the end. Let us treat each moment as precious. Give us a clear mind and a sober spirit so that we may pray for what is needed in your world. Thank you for never forgetting us. Some of us have been waiting for a long time. Waiting for dreams to manifest into reality. Give us the clarity and the faith to know that the wait is over. We receive your blessings. In Jesus' name, amen.

DAY 40

For The Millions

Hebrews 12:1a - (NRSV) - *Therefore, since we are surrounded by such a great cloud of witnesses, let us throw off everything that hinders and the sin that so easily entangles. And let us run with perseverance the race marked out for us…*

Let's face it. The uniqueness of this movie is not simply that it has a cast full of Black people. We've seen movies before that were full of Black folk, but the uniqueness of the Black Panther is that it has stamped its magnificent cultural footprint into the sand of cinematic history and into our own lives. Not only is it about Black people, but it is about what it means to be Black — what it means to be people of African descent. If ever there was a time when a movie like this is necessary, it is now. We live in a political climate that is fraught with chaos, where the stated mission, "Make America Great Again" is a euphemism for "Take America Back to Jim Crow Again." Living in a world where we are hard-pressed to find a country not touched by western colonization and influence, to witness a land (as mythical as the country may be) on the big screen that is not only untouched by colonization but is the most advanced place on earth, helps give endless possibilities to the impressionable minds of our young people.

On the heels of the President of the United States of America calling Haiti and African countries "sh*thole countries", the world needs a reminder that Africa is the cradle of civilization. It is in Africa where the greatest monuments and structures known to humanity were built. It is there where our people learned to treat ailments using the resources of the earth and where the greatest philosophers and griots were found.

Therefore, "since we are surrounded by such a great cloud of witnesses (ancestors), let us throw off everything that hinders and the sin (trespasses and offenses) that so easily entangles..."[20] Let us never look back or slow down. Let us never forget who we are. We do it in memory of the millions of

---

[20] Hebrews 12:1

ancestors whose names we will never know; who crossed the Atlantic in the bowels of slave ships and for the many more who spirits lay at the bottom of the ocean. We press forth in memory of the millions of ancestors who marched for the right to live as well as the right to vote. We succeed for the millions of ancestors who were lynched and burned. We are unstoppable for the millions of mothers, fathers, uncles, aunts, brothers, sisters, sons and daughters who we will never know because they were taken from us. For those of us who will never know our true names or our true family tree—for the millions of ancestors who were raped and for families who were separated, we stand and declare that we're still here. God has made us stronger and wiser. Now let us throw off everything that hinders us and run life's race, accepting nothing less than victory in Jesus Christ!

Prayer

"God of our weary years, God of our silent tears,
Thou Who hast brought us thus far on the way;
Thou Who hast by Thy might, led us into the light,

Keep us forever in the path, we pray."[21]

Lord, we thank you for the millions of ancestors who have gone before us. We know that it is by your power and guidance that we stand on their shoulders today. Let us not take lightly the sacrifices that have been made. When we grow weary, strengthen us and remind us of the road that has been already been forged for us. Thank you for the ancestors.

Now, "lest our feet stray from the places our God, where we met Thee. Lest our hearts, drunk with the wine of the world, we forget Thee. Shadowed beneath Thy hand, may we forever stand, true to our God, true to our native land."[22] *In Jesus' name, amen.*

---

[21] Taken from "Lift Every Voice And Sing" also known as the "Negro National Anthem" or the "Black National Anthem, written by James Weldon Johnson in 1900.

[22] Final words in "Lift Every Voice"

Closing Thoughts

After seeing the movie, someone asked the question, who was the real villain? Was it Ulysses Klaus? Was it Eric Killmonger. My personal opinion is that the villain was not a person. Rather the villain was a misdeed— a missed opportunity with horrific and critical consequences. We recall when T'Challa meets his father in the 'after-realm' and demands to know why his cousin, Killmonger, whose real name is N'Jadaka, was left behind in Oakland, California. Why didn't T'Chaka bring N'Jadaka back to Wakanda with him? T'Chaka responds to T'Challa, "It was the truth I chose to omit." I propose that the omission of the truths in our lives, as individuals and as a community, is the real villain. We choose to omit the inconvenient truths and to accept those which are convenient and which align with our personal goals. When we choose to omit the truths in our lives and in our society, we create products of misunderstanding that can be dangerous—such as N'Jadaka/Killmonger. I believe that N'Jadaka was a victim more than a villain. But due to his victimization as a result of the omission of the truth, he became a danger to himself and to others. It is a reminder that not only do we all have the ability to choose, but that our choices are important.

The question for all of us is where do we stand on issues and with decisions which are inconvenient, but which beg our wrestling with while searching for what is true and for what is just. Let us not only *seek* the truth. But once found, let us *embrace* the truth

---

I pray that as you travel on life's journey that you will collide with the goodness and beauty of God in everything that you do. If you like this book, please let somebody else know. For more information or if you wish to support my work in ministry, please visit lisadjenkins.org. In the meantime, remain unstoppable, always operating in God's power and authority!

About The Author

Rev. Lisa D. Jenkins is the senior pastor of the St. Matthew's Baptist Church of Harlem. She is also an Adjunct Lecturer of multicultural studies with the City University of New York, and has taught Biblical Exegesis, New Testament Studies and the Politics of Jesus at New York Theological Seminary. She is currently a Facilitator for Fuller Theological Seminary's Micah Group Program. Rev. Jenkins received her B.S. in Speech Communications from Pace University and her M.Div. from New York Theological Seminary and is currently a doctoral student at McCormick Theological Seminary in Chicago. Rev. Jenkins is an advocate for both children and adults with ADHD. She is the mother of one son. All of this sounds very serious, but Rev. J. is actually a very cool and fun person who believes strongly in Jesus, justice and the power of laughter.

www.lisadjenkins.org

Made in the USA
Middletown, DE
25 May 2018